D1377231

THE EAST INDIANS AND THE PAKISTANIS IN AMERICA

The IN AMERICA *Series*

THE EAST INDIANS
AND THE PAKISTANIS IN AMERICA

LEONA B. BAGAI

Published by
Lerner Publications Company
Minneapolis, Minnesota

. . . CONTENTS . . .

PART I. India and America

  1. *The Beginning*... 7
  2. *The Exchange of Ideas and Ideals*......................... 8

PART II. The Background of the East Indians

  1. *The People and the Country*.............................. 13
  2. *The British Come to India*............................... 15

PART III. The Journey to America Begins

  1. *The Immigrant*.. 19
  2. *The Transition*... 19
  3. *The Forerunners*.. 24

PART IV. The Pioneers

  1. *A Bengali Brings India's Philosophies to America*....... 25
  2. *The Sikhs Come to Farm in California*................... 28
  3. *A Gujarati Fights for Citizenship in America*.......... 30
  4. *A Hindu from the United Provinces Wins the Pulitzer Prize*..... 32
  5. *The Fight for Citizenship and Independence*............ 34
  6. *A Sikh Becomes the First Asian Elected to Congress*.... 35
  7. *A Sindhi Merchant's Success and Generosity*........... 37

PART V. Pakistan Is Born

  1. *Conflicts*... 41
  2. *Muslim Pioneers in America*............................ 42
  3. *Recent Residents*...................................... 46

PART VI. East Indian Immigration Since 1947

  1. *The Students*.. 49
  2. *Contributions to Science, Industry, and Medicine*...... 51
  3. *Contributions to the Arts and Education*............... 54
  4. *Contributions in Agriculture*.......................... 58
  5. *Property and Business*................................. 58

Conclusion... 59

Siva is the second god of the three who make up Brahman, the single essential Hindu god, or Spirit. The first is Brahma, the creator, and the third is Vishnu, the preserver. Hindus believe that Siva destroys in order to make room for new life, an idea which is suggested by the dancing god within the circle. This thirteenth century bronze sculpture from India is in the collection of the Denver Art Museum.

Illustration from a *Ragmala*, a set of poems describing the 36 musical modes. This miniature, painted on paper, dates from about 1630 and is in the collection of the Museum of Fine Arts in Boston.

PART I

India and America

1. *The Beginning*

America owes its discovery to India. In the fifteenth century India was a great industrial and manufacturing nation. Her delicate muslins, fine linens, woolens, and silks were world famous. India also produced splendid jewelry and pottery, porcelains and ceramics. Her spices made European dishes more tasty. America was accidentally discovered when Europeans tried to find a quicker means of obtaining these luxuries.

Columbus thought he had come upon India by sailing west. He named the native people found on the North American continent "Indians," and that error still creates confusion today. That is why when we say "Indian" we must precede it with the proper term: *East Indian* for people from India and the islands nearby; *West Indian* for people from the islands lying between North and South America; and *American Indian* for the original natives of our land.

Walt Whitman (1819-1892). Whitman's familiarity with Hindu beliefs may be seen in his collection of poems, *Leaves of Grass*. This painting of Whitman by Thomas Eakins is in the collection of the Pennsylvania Academy of the Fine Arts.

2. *The Exchange of Ideas and Ideals*

Three hundred years after Columbus's discovery of the New World, there was enough commerce between India and America to warrant an American consul in Calcutta. Ships from the new United States sailed to Indian ports in the years after the American Revolution. In a trading cycle profitable to both countries, America shipped precious ice to India and returned with rare spices, silks, and the literature of the East.

Volumes of India's poetry, philosophy, and religion found their way into the libraries of the educated and cultured people of New England, affecting the writers of that time. The well-known philosopher and writer, Ralph Waldo Emerson, had many books from India in his personal library, including the *Bhagvad Gita*, a Hindu book about devotion and faith. When Emerson wrote: "I am the doubter and the doubt/and I am the hymn the Brahmin sings," he was reflecting the unity of life as the Hindu sees it.

Walt Whitman, a famous poet of the nineteenth century, expressed the infinite world within oneself. He incorporated many basic Hindu ideas in his *Leaves of Grass*.

8

Like Emerson, Henry David Thoreau was a distinguished American writer and thinker. He loved solitude and the discipline of meditation. For over two years he lived close to nature at Walden Pond. His life there was similar to that of an Indian *yogi*, or disciplined, meditative person seeking harmony with Brahma, the supreme god of the Hindu religion.

In the twentieth century Mahatma Gandhi, one of India's great leaders, read the writings of Thoreau and was very much impressed with his essay, "On the Duty of Civil Disobedience." Thoreau had written this after spending a night in jail when he refused to pay his poll tax. He felt that his tax money was being used for a needless war in Mexico.

In 1930 Gandhi wanted to protest England's monopoly of the manufacture of salt and the heavy tax Indians had to pay on the salt. He marched 200 miles to the sea, where he boiled ocean water to make salt illegally. He urged the people of India to repeat his act of civil disobedience. Millions followed him, and over 60,000 East Indians, including Gandhi, were jailed.

Gandhi had borrowed from Thoreau the idea of quiet, conscientious protest. Later Gandhi extended his methods of protest against his English rulers to include "nonviolence." No matter how brutally the British soldiers treated the East Indians, they were to respond with compassion and were not to fight back, in hopes of

Henry David Thoreau (1817-1862) had studied the Hindu classics and was to a certain extent influenced by them in his writing and in his way of life. Mahatma Gandhi, in turn, was deeply impressed by Thoreau's essay, "On the Duty of Civil Disobedience."

changing their ruler's mind. This method of responding to injustices with quiet, understanding protest was one of the means by which India achieved independence from England.

In America, a portrait of Gandhi hangs in the living room of Dr. Martin Luther King, Jr. Reverend King has studied, and in the last decade put into action, Gandhi's methods of moral protest. He has used nonviolent marches to protest racial segregation in Birmingham, Alabama and in his campaigns for voter-registration in Selma, Alabama and fair housing in Chicago. These marches drew attention to injustices. Although they were met by tear gas, rocks, and insults, the marchers were peaceable and won many of their points.

India and America are the two largest democracies in the world. Individual freedom is one of the important ideals they have in common. Both countries gained their independence from England. Both contain a large number of varied groups and types of people. Their citizens are free to follow their individual customs and religions, and those religions are kept separate from the government.

It is interesting to compare two great leaders of the United States and India, Abraham Lincoln and Mahatma Gandhi. Both yearned for the unification of their country, Lincoln at the time of the Civil War and Gandhi at the time of the partition of India and

Abraham Lincoln (1812-1865). There are many parallels between his life and that of Mahatma Gandhi, the great Indian leader. Indians, in their struggle for liberty, have had a special regard for Lincoln.

Mohandas K. Gandhi (1869-1948) was called *Mahatma* (Great Soul) by the people of India. A Hindu, he was educated in India and in London, and went to South Africa as a young lawyer in 1893. He remained there until 1915, using new methods of nonviolence to help the Indian minority gain reforms. After his return to India he became a leader in the movement for independence. He favored widespread use of passive resistance; as an individual, he fasted and underwent imprisonment in order to influence the British and to unify his own people. In January 1948, less than a year after independence, Gandhi was shot and killed by a Hindu who resented his belief in tolerance of all religions.

Pakistan. Both worked for the betterment of people of the lowest social levels, Lincoln for the Negro slaves and Gandhi for the caste of untouchables. Both were considered by their critics to be unrealistic idealists, ugly and awkward. Both were assassinated.

Mahatma Gandhi was honored with a United States postage stamp issued on January 26, 1961, the eleventh anniversary of India's becoming a republic. India honored Abraham Lincoln with a stamp issued on April 15, 1965, the 100th anniversary of Lincoln's assassination.

Many parts of India's constitution are based on the constitution of the United States. India's citizens have the rights of social, economic, and political justice. They also have liberty of thought, expression, and worship.

Thus, India and America, though half a world apart, have for a long time exchanged concepts of a more perfect society for mankind. Immigrants from India today feel quite at home in America's climate of freedom and opportunity.

An American postage stamp (left) honoring Mahatma Gandhi was issued on January 26, 1961, India's Republic Day. Abraham Lincoln appears on an Indian stamp (right) issued on April 15, 1965, the 100th anniversary of his assassination.

The Great Mosque in Delhi. Shah Jahan, a Mogul emperor, directed the building of this mosque and of other temples and palaces at Delhi in the mid-seventeenth century. Delhi was capital of India from 1912 until 1931 when the government moved to New Delhi, a suburb of the old city. New Delhi remained capital when India became independent in 1947.

PART II

The Background of the East Indians

1. *The People and the Country*

India is a subcontinent, shaped somewhat like our state of Texas. It encompasses an area of 1,261,597 square miles, or about half that of the United States. The Arabian Sea, the Indian Ocean, and the Bay of Bengal lie to the west, south, and east of India. Its northern borders touch Pakistan, China, and Burma. Pakistan was a part of India until after the Second World War.

India's northern borders contain the highest mountains in the world, the Himalayas. The country also has very dry, hot deserts and areas that receive as much as 424 inches of rain a year. There are tropical forests, plains, and high rocky plateaus within its borders.

The geographical contrasts, the climate, and the people and their cultures in India are varied and rich. It is true that India has tigers and jungles, but it also has steel mills and factories, and it is second, next to Japan, in the production of motion pictures. India

Vishnu, the third aspect of the Hindu god Brahman. Vishnu is known as the preserver, and is worshipped by his followers as a god of love. This bronze sculpture, from the fourteenth or fifteenth century, is in the Denver Art Museum.

also has large cities with traffic problems and smog, just as the United States does.

India's history dates back more than 5,000 years. There were people living in the Indus Valley in what is now West Pakistan in 2500 B.C. Their alphabet still has not been deciphered. As far as we know, the original natives of India were Dravidians. About 1500 B.C. the Aryans came from Europe through India's northwest mountain passes. Later the Persians, Greeks, Huns, Arabs, Turks, Mongols, and Moguls also came. This last group brought their Muslim religion and a series of rulers who fashioned some of India's most beautiful architecture. In 1947 Muslims formed the modern country of Pakistan.

Through assimilation of their invaders, the people of India have inherited a variety of complexions, from the very fair to the very dark. People from North India, especially Kashmir, may even have blue eyes. Stature of the East Indians ranges from thin delicacy to sturdy, broad frames; features, from large eyes and sharp noses to the slanted eyes and flat noses of the people related to Mongolian invaders.

It is very difficult to recognize an East Indian or Pakistani in America. He may be very fair-skinned. Or he may look as though he came from one of the countries on the Mediterranean Sea. He might be mistaken for a Mexican or even an American Indian. Only the Sikh from northwest India is easily recognizable when he wears his turban, beard, and steel bracelet. And today many less orthodox Sikhs have discarded these.

Mr. and Mrs. Sarwan Singh Gill of San Francisco. Mr. Gill is a modern Sikh, and wears only the steel bracelet.

2. *The British Come to India*

Until the eighteenth century India absorbed the peoples and religions that came to her country. Muslims and Hindus intermarried and many were converted to the other's religion. A group called the Parsees fled from Persia and found refuge in the city of Bombay, eventually becoming one of the wealthiest groups there.

Jews left their persecutors in the Middle East and settled along India's west coast. As different as all these groups were, they learned to live side by side and to conduct their business and family lives in peace.

The British came to India as a commercial venture. The East India Company set up offices in the ports of India, making treaties or making war as they progressed inland, whichever was more advantageous. The East India Company became so prosperous that its stock rose to $32,000 a share. In 10 years alone, $30,000,000 was taken out of India in taxes and tributes. After 1857 all of India became Britain's and she was officially a crown colony.

Robert Clive (1725-1774) joined the East India Company as a clerk in 1743 and later became a commander in the company's armed services. England and France were struggling at this time for control of India, and Clive's troops defeated the French and Indians in several important battles. (Below) British soldiers at the Battle of Plassey, June 1757. Clive's victory at Plassey gave Britain control of the rich province of Bengal and marked the end of French competition in India.

The British transport reinforcements to Delhi during the Sepoy Rebellion in 1857. The Sepoys were Indian soldiers in the army of the British East India Company. Although a long chain of dissatisfactions caused them to rebel, the immediate reason was the British order that they bite off the ends of their cartridges, which were greased with cow or hog fat. Neither Hindus nor Muslims would do this. The rebellion, which spread through northern India, was suppressed by the British. As a result, the British government abolished the East India Company and assumed direct control of India, governing through a viceroy and council appointed by the queen. Gradually, in the twentieth century, Indians were included in the government but were always subject to the viceroy's veto.

Slowly, India's economy suffered and her people became poorer and poorer. Exports dwindled as England put an 80 percent tariff on India's textiles, while India was compelled to admit English textiles duty-free.

India's culture also suffered when England closed the village schools and made English compulsory in city schools. British officials kept strictly apart from Indians, socially. Indians were not allowed to rise higher than to clerical positions in the intricate system of government administration and law that England imported to rule this country.

Indians began to rebel against this imposed authority, especially after England suddenly partitioned the state of Bengal, dividing Hindu and Muslim communities. An Indian National Congress was formed in 1885. As England became aware of the changing temper of the people, repressive measures such as the Rowlatt Act were passed. Under this law a person could be arrested for owning a scrap of writing that advocated freedom for India.

17

Sepoy troops in the British army, 1942.

During this time Gandhi formulated his ideas on nonviolent resistance. Nevertheless, riots took place and English officials were bombed by revolutionary patriots.

In the Punjab region in northwest India, on April 15, 1919, a British general and his men opened fire on an unarmed crowd of men, women, and children celebrating a religious festival. They did not cease firing until all the ammunition was used. The people were in a walled park, known as Jallianwala Bagh, and were unable to escape. About 1,500 were killed or wounded. This massacre so shocked and united India that it is said "The British Empire died at the Jallianwala Bagh."

Migration to America was an escape from this kind of tyranny.

PART III

The Journey to America Begins

1. *The Immigrant*

It was not an easy thing to leave India for America. It took a great deal of money, and India's middle and upper classes had always been a very tiny percent of her population. Also, people with a cultural history thousands of years old have many rules of social behavior — governing marriage, occupation, diet, and methods of worship — that are difficult, if not impossible, to follow in strange lands.

Thus, it took a very courageous, flexible, financially independent person to make the trip to the United States. Those having the money to travel were few. Those having the initiative to do so were fewer still.

2. *The Transition*

The three main groups of East Indians who came to America were religious ones: Hindu, Muslim, and Sikh. The Sikhs comprised over half of those who came; the Muslims, one-third. Perhaps fewer Hindus came because they had to alter so many of their ways of life. The Hindu had to make up his mind to forget his background of caste, or social position.

In today's India caste rules are slowly breaking down, and no one can be excluded from a job or government position because of them. But when India's people first came to America, caste was a way of life and the basis of India's ancient social structure.

The four traditional castes of India.

Sudras (left), the lowest caste, known as "untouchables."

Brahmins (right), the highest caste—priests, scholars, and teachers.

Vaisyas (left), a middle caste— merchants and farmers.

Kshatriyas (right), the second highest caste— rulers and soldiers.

There were four traditional castes. The highest were called *Brahmins.* They were priests, scholars, and teachers. The next highest were called *Kshatriyas.* This group was made up of rulers, generals, and soldiers. The next were called *Vaisyas,* and they were landlords, shopkeepers, and farmers. The lowest caste were *Sudras,* in modern times called "untouchables." They were barbers, potters, and servants who did the lowest, dirtiest tasks.

The Hindus believe in reincarnation, or the idea that a man's soul does not die, but passes from one life to another. It was thought that whatever caste a person was born into was the result of his past life. If he had been a good person, he was born into a high caste. If he became a better person, he would be born into a higher caste in his next life. It was believed that one should not attempt to change castes in this life. Each caste had strict rules that determined one's occupation and whom one might marry, be friends with, or even eat with.

When a Hindu came to America he was faced with many adjustments. He was uncertain about the kind of job he might get. He might have to wash dishes or do janitor's work before getting the job he was qualified for, such as teaching. He could not easily tell, in America, what position a man had, and therefore whether to look up to him or to avoid him. Caste would certainly have to be forgotten in a land where rich men's sons took summer jobs digging ditches and newsboys rose to become industrialists. It was this very challenge of individual freedom that attracted so many of India's most adaptable, ambitious, and intelligent people to America.

Dietary habits also presented a problem. In India the Hindu aversion to taking life led to vegetarianism. The orthodox Hindu did not eat any animal, fish, or fowl. The most orthodox did not even eat eggs. Eating beef was especially repugnant to the Hindu as the cow was considered sacred. However, the hamburger became a regular part of the diet of many an East Indian student in America on a low budget.

21

The Muslim found fewer adjustments to make in America. His religion taught him equality and brotherhood, and he could easily obtain a good diet without including the pork or alcohol forbidden him. The Muslim woman had to adjust to a more public life, however. In India, *purdah*, an elaborate system of keeping women hidden from view, was observed. Women were confined to their homes. Veils were worn over the face in the presence of men in the family, other than the husband. If women had to go out they wore a *burka*, or heavy covering from head to foot, with little slits to peep through.

These Hindu women of the Punjab remained in India when their husbands emigrated to America in 1918. Because of restrictive American immigration laws of the 1920's, many were unable to join their husbands.

Mrs. Kala Chandra Bagai, a Sikh, was one of the seven pioneer women who came to America from India before World War I.

The sturdy Sikh farmers who came to the United States found little trouble adjusting to American ways. Most became farmers here also. In India farming was done on small amounts of land continually growing smaller as sons and grandsons divided the family property. The Sikhs were delighted with the vast amounts of space still available in this country.

The loose, comfortable clothing worn by the men of all three groups in India was exchanged for the American business suit, starched shirt, and tie. Shoes were a distinct discomfort compared to the loose, airy sandals worn in India.

The Hindu woman had many adjustments to make. Her change to western clothes was very difficult after wearing the *sari*, a six-yard length of material draped loosely around the body, over a petticoat and small blouse. This dress covered her legs. Her hair had probably never been cut in her life and had been worn in a plait or bun. Western styles of short dresses, bare arms, and short hair seemed to her altogether immodest.

The woman from India learned to mix white and wheat flour to obtain a special blend she preferred for her daily *chapatis*, a bread somewhat heavier than Mexican tortillas. And the Sikh farmers in California soon provided her with the varieties of lentils and beans needed to substitute for meat.

More importantly, the woman from India realized that her family's future would be changed. Sikhs, Hindus, and Muslims have the joint-family system. Grown brothers and their wives live in the same house with the father and mother. The sisters of the family go to live in the household of their husband. Cousins are raised like brothers, and family life is very warm and satisfying. Everyone knows everyone's business and shares everyone's problems.

The East Indian woman realized that in America she would have to face problems with only her husband's guidance, and perhaps he too was unused to making decisions on his own, particularly if he was the youngest of many sons in a large household. In India other women in her family had helped to raise her children. Also, with so many poor in India needing work she had had servants to help with the household. If her children married independently in America, into a family whose background was unknown, it would mean a total break with past customs. So severely were these changes regarded that only seven East Indian women came to America before World War I.

3. The Forerunners

According to immigration statistics the first East Indian arrived in America in 1820. We do not know who he was, but he might have been a seaman or a visitor on one of the Boston ships returning from India. One of the first merchants to come to the United States was Mr. Bungara, a Parsee, who brought fine India brass to California in 1895.

In the late nineteenth century East Indians began to go to England for their higher education. A few continued on to visit the United States and then remained.

Vedanta Temple in Hollywood, California.

PART IV

The Pioneers

1. *A Bengali Brings India's Philosophies to America*

For more than 100 years America had enjoyed India's written philosophies. In 1893 the people of the United States heard them spoken in person by a dynamic young man from Bengal in eastern India.

Swami Vivekananda came to the Parliament of Religions at the World's Columbian Exposition in Chicago in September 1893. His opening address began, "Sisters and Brothers of America . . ." The audience of 7,000 broke into spontaneous applause and gave him a standing ovation. With those words he had conveyed to them the unity of mankind and the purpose of the convention. He had, after all, come from the most distant part of the earth at a time when it took months to travel, not days. His eloquence and enthusiasm made him one of the most popular speakers in this assembly of religious leaders from all over the world.

He gave talks on Vedanta philosophy, the basic ideas of Hindus on the nature of the soul and man's destiny. One Vedantic principle is that all religions speak the same truths and lead to the same

25

realization of God, an especially appropriate message for this gathering.

During his several visits Swami Vivekananda gave lectures throughout the United States. He found a ready audience, for Bulfinch's *Age of Fable*, which included some Hindu mythology, was a popular family and school book, and Sir Edwin Arnold's *Light of Asia* was well-known. An American Oriental Society had been founded in 1842, and Sanskrit had been taught at Yale since 1840 and at Harvard since 1872. Vivekananda was offered full professorships at both Harvard and Columbia Universities, but he declined. He had come to America for a definite purpose, formed in India.

The Swami was born Narendranath Datta in 1863 in Calcutta in the Indian state of Bengal, which was at that time the center of a cultural reawakening — a period of great activity among poets, painters, and social reformers. At 18, Naren was a leader among his college classmates. He could sing and play musical instruments and was a good scholar and athlete. One day he was invited to sing at a gathering. There he met Ramakrishna, who became his spiritual *guru*, or teacher.

For five years, until Ramakrishna's death, Naren underwent a spiritual growth from which he emerged Swami Vivekananda. In India a swami is the same as a monk. He has taken certain religious vows and has been given a name by his teacher indicating his best qualities. Vivekananda in Sanskrit means "discrimination and peace through enlightenment."

After Ramakrishna's death in 1886, Vivekananda gathered 15 monks together and formed the Ramakrishna Order. For a time they wandered throughout India, visiting places of pilgrimage and eating only what they were given by the wealthy or by the poor.

From these travels Vivekananda saw that religion would do India no good until her social conditions could be improved. He decided to bring India's spiritual messages to the United States, and there to seek financial help and learn ways of action.

"America is a good training ground to bring out all that is in a man," Vivekananda once said. In 1894, one year after he first came to America, he founded the first Vedanta Center in New York. With funds from America he started the first of the Ramakrishna Missions in India.

Today the missions have their own high schools, industrial and agricultural schools, hospitals, a college, a library, and a publishing house. In America the Vedanta Centers number over a dozen in major cities from coast to coast. They also have a publishing house in Hollywood.

Vedantic thought has influenced many American philosophers and historians, among them Aldous Huxley, Will Durant, and Christopher Isherwood. The scientists Albert Einstein and Robert Oppenheimer also took a deep interest in the philosophies of India.

Swami Vivekananda died at 39 years of age near Calcutta in 1902. His brief and brilliant service to brotherhood created a lasting link between India and America.

Swami Vivekananda spoke at the Parliament of Religions in 1893 and later founded the first Vedanta Center in America.

2. *The Sikhs Come to Farm in California*

Although more than half of the people who have come to America from India are Sikhs, in India they form less than two percent of the population. They are an important two percent, however, because of their vigor and initiative.

Sikhs come from the Punjab, a northwest region that has five main rivers. Some of the Punjab is now a part of West Pakistan. The rest is an Indian state. When India and Pakistan were divided, most Sikhs left Pakistan to settle near Amritsar, India where their Golden Temple is located.

The Sikh religion is a new one in India compared to the Hindu and Muslim faiths. It was founded by Guru Nanak, a religious teacher who lived in the fifteenth century. He tried to combine the best parts of the Hindu and Muslim religions, to bring the two peoples closer together. The *Garanth,* or Sikh bible, is dedicated to unity, truth, and one God.

A religious male Sikh adheres to the five K's: *Kesh*—hair and beard uncut; *Kungha*—comb in the hair; *Kuchha*—the shorts the men wear; *Kara*—the steel bracelet; and *Kirpan*—the sword worn at the belt. In America, however, most Sikhs retain only the steel bracelet and uncut hair and beard. A turban is wound around the long hair. Many modern Sikhs are clean-shaven and do not wear a turban.

Often tall, the Sikhs are good-natured and independent. The majority of Sikhs in India are farmers. Their community has produced some of the finest fighters in the British army. Since India's independence they have defended her borders valiantly against both China and Pakistan.

A severe drought from 1898 to 1902 brought starvation to the Punjab region, and in a desperate move many Sikhs emigrated to America. Between 1900 and 1910 almost 5,000 Sikh men came to California. Because of their turbans they were called "rag heads" by the local residents. They were not allowed to enter stores or rent rooms. Many of them camped in the woods, migrating from place to place as crops needed their labor. Eighteen cents an hour was a common wage for agricultural work.

Sikhs were experienced farmers of sugar cane, corn, cotton,

and melons in India, and their talents were soon recognized. They were sought for their skilled handling of fig orchards and vineyards around Fresno, and were also hired in the rice lands near Sacramento. Many became farm managers and labor contractors. The Western Pacific employed many "Hindoos," as all people from India were termed at that time, to build its railroad. And the lumber mills of Seattle hired Sikhs for $1.50 a day.

As a whole, however, the Sikhs preferred orchard and agricultural work. It was not long before they improved their lot, and by 1918 over 50,000 acres of rice land alone in California were farmed by Sikhs from India.

Sikh communities in both Stockton and El Centro, California built temples. Next to them they built kitchens and dormitories, providing a place for worship, school, and community gatherings, and a rest house for male travelers who were ill or without money. Sikh communities celebrate holidays with a *langar*, providing free food for the hundreds of people assembled. During these times the Garanth, or holy book, is read from beginning to end, in relays.

The Sikhs were the people celebrating their spring festival at Jallianwala Bagh when they were fired upon by the British general. After that event many of the men decided to emigrate to America and to return later for their families. They found, however, after

A group of lumber mill workers celebrate the Fourth of July, 1920 with an American flag and their own version of India's flag. All are Sikhs from the Punjab who came to work in Seattle, Washington.

attaining some financial success in America, that they could not bring their wives and children to the United States because of new immigration laws rejecting Orientals. This is one of the reasons the East Indian population in America has remained so small. Many of the East Indian men of this generation remained bachelors. A few of them married women from Mexico who lived in their farming communities.

After the first flood of immigration from the Punjab, the stream of people coming from India slowed to a trickle. Between 1931 and 1940 only 496 East Indians entered the United States because of restrictive immigration laws. Naturalization laws had also been changed. East Indians were now denied citizenship.

3. *A Gujarati Fights for Citizenship in America*

Because he had been a second-class citizen in India under British rule, the East Indian felt deeply the denial of citizenship in America. One of the few who gained and retained his American citizenship was Dr. Sakaram Ganesh Pandit.

Dr. Pandit was born in 1875 in the state of Gujarat in western India. Dr. Pandit was a Hindu of the highest caste, a Chitpavan Brahmin. As a child he felt the weight of British oppression, for children were treated as severely as adults if they demonstrated any national feelings.

Dr. Pandit received his bachelor of arts degree from the University of Bombay, majoring in logic, moral philosophy, and English and Sanskrit literature. The Hindu University at Dharwar awarded him the special degree of doctor of education and philosophy. In 1906 he left India to lecture in Paris and London. Later that year he arrived in New York.

In American universities Dr. Pandit lectured on Sanskrit literature, logic, religion, and philosophy. He did postgraduate work at the University of Chicago and after studying law in Los Angeles, was admitted to the bar in 1917. For many years he both practiced and taught law in Los Angeles.

Dr. Pandit became a citizen of the United States in 1914. Nine years later, the government tried to cancel his certificate of naturalization. This was because of American immigration and naturalization laws. The first United States naturalization law, passed in 1790, stated that any alien could become a citizen if he were a "free white person." This excluded Negroes and American Indians, as the former were slaves and the latter were considered enemies.

Before 1860 Japanese, East Indians, and over 1,000 Chinese were naturalized. But people began to fear that cheap Chinese labor would flood the market and leave no jobs for Americans. In 1882 Congress suspended Chinese labor immigration for 10 years and excluded the Chinese from citizenship. Soon restrictive legislation required that an applicant prove himself a "white person" to become a citizen.

Dr. Pandit had obtained his citizenship in 1914 on the grounds that he *was* a white person, since East Indians belonged to the Aryan race. Although the government objected, he won his case

Dr. Sakaram Ganesh Pandit, in 1923. A lawyer and scholar, he was one of the very few East Indians who were able to gain and retain American citizenship prior to passage of the Luce-Cellar Bill in 1946.

and his citizenship. However, in 1923 the United States Government suddenly cancelled the recently obtained citizenship of a Sikh gentleman. The grounds were that he had obtained his citizenship under false pretenses; that he was not white. The judge ruled that the term "white" related not to scientific or ethnological terms but to terms of "the man on the street." To the average man on the street, the judge contended, this Sikh gentleman with his turban looked different from the majority of people in the community who had come from Europe to settle in America.

This 1923 court ruling set off proceedings by the government against about 70 East Indians who had been naturalized during the preceding 15 years, including Dr. Pandit. Like the others, Dr. Pandit had much to lose if he lost the citizenship that had been his for nine years. He had married an American citizen in 1920, and she would lose her citizenship if he lost his. He had become a lawyer and a notary public and would not be able to practice either profession if he were to lose his citizenship. He and his wife had bought a home and additional land in Imperial Valley, California, and the title to both would be lost, for noncitizens could not own property. He had also passed on to other family members in India title to 400 acres of land there, since he expected to spend the rest of his life in America as an American citizen.

As a lawyer, Dr. Pandit had an advantage in pursuing his case through the courts. For four years he fought and in 1927 he won a final decision in his favor in the Supreme Court. Dr. Pandit was one of the few East Indians allowed to remain a citizen of the United States. Fifteen similar cases pending were dismissed.

4. A Hindu from the United Provinces Wins the Pulitzer Prize

During the last week of August 1912, a boat left Yokahama, Japan. Although it had a rough and stormy passage and was delayed by heavy autumn fog, the boat finally entered San Francisco harbor. There was no Golden Gate Bridge then. Suddenly the skies cleared and the sinking sun illumined the Bay Cities and San Francisco.

Houses and beautiful office buildings on terraces reflected the sunlight in countless patterns aglow—like a crown set with dazzling jewels. The unexpected newness of everything—the clean air, the orange-yellow ferry boat to Berkeley, the bright children and healthy, attractive women, the beautiful cities and wide streets—filled me with the joy of discovery. The old world of India I'd left behind had been one of crowded cities, policemen, beggars, a few very arrogant rich and many humble poor.

My first impression of America was of well-being, humor and hopefulness. In America I found an equality I had not even conceived before. No social classes; no castes.

These are the memories of an East Indian, Gobind Behari Lal, who has gained unusual success and respect in America. Gobind was born in the city of Delhi in 1889. He was an early rebel, and at 11 he gave lectures to a boys' club on the abolition of the caste system and the custom of *purdah*.

Gobind Behari Lal received a Pulitzer Prize for scientific journalism in 1937.

In 1910, from a vantage point of 8,000 feet in the Himalayan mountains, Gobind saw Halley's Comet streak across the sky. This experience aroused his lifelong interest in science.

After receiving his master of arts degree at St. Stephans College at the University of the Punjab, Gobind became assistant professor of general science at the Hindu College of the same university. Then he came to America where he did postgraduate work at the University of California in Berkeley.

From 1925 to 1930 Dr. Lal was a feature writer for the *San Francisco Examiner*. He was then science editor for Universal Service, International News Service, and *American Weekly*. In 1937 he received the Pulitzer Prize for scientific journalism.

Dr. Lal has received many other awards of recognition. He was a Watumull Foundation Research Fellow at Columbia University. He won the George Westinghouse Distinguished Science Writer's Award in 1946 and the Taraknath Das Foundation Prize at Columbia University in 1958. He is the author of several scientific books and has been science editor *emeritus*, Hearst Newspapers, since 1954.

5. *The Fight for Citizenship and Independence*

America has always given refuge to homeless patriots who have struggled for freedom in their native lands. Revolutionaries working for India's independence came to America as early as 1898. Some East Indians led an exile's life in America for as long as 40 years. America benefited from their cultural contributions. One of the most prominent was Dr. Syud Hossain.

Dr. Hossain was born in Bengal, the son of a Muslin governor. As a young man he helped edit the *Bombay Chronicle*. Renouncing family ties, he joined Gandhi's movement in 1917.

Syud Hossain came to America in 1923 from the Hague Conference. He was the foremost proponent of Gandhi's ideals in the United States. At the University of Southern California he lectured intermittently on the history and civilization of India. Until 1947, as chairman of the National Committee for India's Independence in Washington, D. C., he answered many of the British Government's arguments against giving India freedom.

Although a Muslim, Dr. Hossain worked tirelessly for India's independence and returned there instead of to Pakistan. He was India's first ambassador to Egypt and died in that country in a plane crash.

During World War II strong pressure was directed against the British for India's freedom. India had contributed the largest volunteer army of all the Allies—over 2,500,000 men. She had also supplied 60,000 Merchant Marines and an Air Force of 300,000 to the British. India had helped keep millions of the world's people free. Now she wanted her own freedom.

A group of Indian patriots was aided by prominent Americans in their work for India's independence. Together they tried to gain India's freedom and citizenship for East Indians in the United States. The two issues were inseparable, for they stood for the dignity and individual worth of the East Indian.

There were two paths open toward obtaining American citizenship for East Indians. One was to obtain a reversal of the former Supreme Court decision which declared East Indians to be non-whites. The second was to have a special bill passed in Congress to permit East Indian citizenship. The second course was decided upon.

On July 3, 1946 the Luce-Celler Bill was signed by President Truman. East Indians were allowed to become citizens, own property, and bring their relatives to America on India's quota so that they too could become citizens.

The following year India gained her independence from England. East Indians had finally obtained first-class citizenship in their own country, too.

6. *A Sikh Becomes the First Asian Elected to Congress*

In his childhood days in the village of Chhajalwadi in the Punjab, Dalip Singh Saund never dreamed that he would become a part of the United States Government. He was the son of a well-to-do family that built canals and railroads for the British Government. After graduating from Punjab University, his family wanted him to go into civil service. But, inspired by the ideals of Lincoln, he was already planning to come to America.

In 1920 Dalip Singh Saund began studies in agriculture at the University of California at Berkeley. During summer vacations he worked in canning plants to finance his education. Shortly after getting his doctorate in mathematics, a subject that came easily to him, he began farming in Imperial Valley, where many of his countrymen had settled.

In 1928 Dalip Saund married Marian Kosa, daughter of a Czech immigrant artist. Under his wife's name, Dalip leased land for ventures in alfalfa farming. These proved successful, but later with more speculative crops Saund went into debt and lost two ranches. He refused to declare bankruptcy, however, and eventually paid off all his debts.

Dalip was one of the few well-educated men in the area and was often called upon for public speaking engagements. At these times he would take his dress suit with him to the fields. At six in the evening he would change into his suit, set the irrigation water for three hours, and go to the Toastmasters' Club. At nine he came back, put on his work clothes, and continued irrigating his crops.

Dalip Singh Saund was the first Asian to serve in the House of Representatives.

On July 3, 1946, when the Luce-Celler Bill was signed, Dalip Singh Saund and the other East Indians in Imperial Valley were jubilant. Their community had sent 215 of their sons to serve in the United States Armed Forces to fight for a land that was now truly their own. Dalip Saund had enlisted the cooperation of nearly 2,000 Indian-born residents in California to get the bill passed.

Dalip now had an opportunity to enter politics. After he received his naturalization papers he was elected a judge in Westmoreland, where he served for four years. He did not escape the sting of prejudice, however. One day in a public restaurant a man called out loudly, "Tell us, if you're elected will you furnish the turbans or will we have to buy them ourselves to appear in court?"

"My friend," Judge Saund replied, "I don't care what a man has on top of his head. All I'm concerned with is what he's got inside of it."

Saund's campaign to run for Congress in 1956 drew national attention. The farming people in his district—of whom the East Indians were decidedly a minority—felt Judge Saund was one of them. They had shared the good crops and the bad, depression days and wartime. They elected him to the United States House of Representatives in an unprecedented display of democracy and fair play.

Ill health forced his retirement after reelection in 1958, but Dalip Singh Saund has had the honor and the satisfaction of being the first East Indian to be elected to Congress.

7. A Sindhi Merchant's Success and Generosity

Gobindram Jhamandas was born on June 26, 1891 in Hyderabad, Sind, an area that is now part of Pakistan. He was the second youngest in a family that included four brothers and five sisters. Goma's father was a brick contractor. However, when Goma was a young boy his father suffered a very severe accident which made him an invalid for the rest of his life. Until the older sons were able to work and support the family, they were dependent on other relatives.

A rich landlord recognized Goma as an intelligent boy and paid a rupee (about 30 cents) a month for his schooling. If his benefactor forgot or paid the money late, Goma had to sit at the foot of the class in humiliation.

Goma's mother was anxious for her sons to receive a good education. When Goma was older she pawned her last remaining ornaments and jewels to pay for his schooling at Karachi University where he studied engineering. After graduating he joined the Sind Engineering Services which managed dams and irrigation on the Indus River. For several years Goma traveled from one project to another on a camel, camping out in tents.

Meanwhile, an older brother, Watumull Jhamandas, had established an import-export business in Manila. Another shop was opened in Honolulu, Hawaii, and in 1917, when Goma was 26 years old he was called there to manage it.

It is the custom in Sind, as in most of India, to use only the first name in public life. Family names are disclosed only at times. of marriage, when they are traced carefully. Thus, Goma's brother had used the name of Mr. Watumull in business. People could not understand why Goma was not Mr. Watumull also, so finally he had his name changed legally to Gobindram Jhamandas Watumull.

G. J. Watumull married in 1922, applied for citizenship, and would have received it in 1923 except for the court ruling against East Indians that year. Mrs. Watumull lost her citizenship until 1931, when the law was changed so that persons married to noncitizens could retain their citizenship.

The Watumull brothers' business grew. They built their own department store and in 1930 opened two more shops. They designed and sold the first raw silk and Hawaiian aloha shirts. About nine years later Mr. Watumull came to Los Angeles for medical treatment, and his family came with him. When the Japanese bombed Pearl Harbor all transportation came into the hands of the military. It was decided that the Watumull family was nonessential to the war effort and they were not allowed transportation back to Hawaii.

Gobindram J. Watumull, merchant and founder of
the Watumull Foundation, which has built educa-
tional links between India and America.

Mr. Watumull opened offices in Los Angeles and New York
and prepared to settle in the United States. He was the financial
mainstay in efforts toward India's freedom promoted by several
groups in America, and also in the struggle for East Indian citizenship. At this time he established the Watumull Foundation.

After the war the Watumulls returned to Hawaii. The work of
the Watumull Foundation gained momentum, bringing 35 highly
qualified men and women to American universities for doctoral
degrees or postgraduate work. Many aspiring young people from
Sind who were left orphans or whose families were penniless at
the time of the partition of India and Pakistan were given scholarships to come to America for study.

The foundation has supported the exchange of noted lecturers, including Dr. John Haynes Holmes, Gandhi's first and greatest American friend, and Dr. Sarvapelli Radhakrishnan, who was President of India. Over 50 American colleges and universities have been given grants for the purchase of books about India. The Watumull Foundation also gives a biennial award through the American Historical Association to the author of the best book about India published in the United States.

G. J. Watumull became an American citizen shortly after the Luce-Celler Bill was passed. He died in August of 1959. The Watumull Foundation, however, assures the continuation of a strong link of ideas and ideals between India and America.

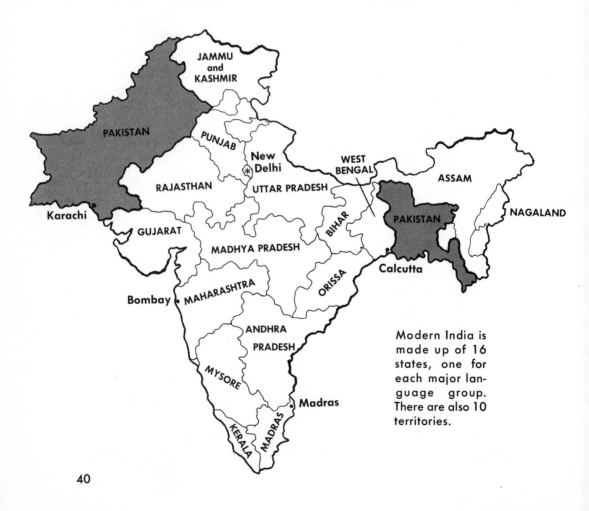

Modern India is made up of 16 states, one for each major language group. There are also 10 territories.

PART V

Pakistan Is Born

1. *Conflicts*

The Muslim League was formed in 1906 to protect Muslim interests against the Hindu majority in India. In 1940 the League, headed by Mohammed Ali Jinnah, began demanding a separate country for the Muslims. When India achieved its freedom from Great Britain in 1947, one of the conditions of the agreement was that the country be partitioned. Two predominantly Muslim areas were carved out of northern India and became East Pakistan and West Pakistan.

Pakistan (meaning the land of the spiritually pure) is an Islamic republic; today 97% of her population is Muslim. It is a unique country because of its division. Over 365,000 square miles in total area, it is divided into two regions more than a thousand miles apart.

Some states were allowed to join either India or Pakistan at the time the country was divided. This arrangement led to many misunderstandings that climaxed in the war between India and Pakistan over the state of Kashmir in 1965.

At the time Pakistan was formed, millions of Muslims moved out of India to live in Pakistan and millions of Hindus fled south to India. As they crossed paths, they killed each other in fear and frustration. Six million lives were lost. Because of this and because of the recent war over Kashmir, there is often bitter feeling today between East Indians and Pakistanis in America.

Immigration from India quadrupled during the decade from 1947 to 1957. In the same period only 20 people came from Pakistan. Because it is a much smaller country than India, Pakistan needed every well-educated Muslim she could keep to help the new country.

Dr. Rais A. Khan, associate professor of political science at Clarion State College in Pennsylvania. He came to the United States as a Fulbright Scholar in 1960 and received his masters and doctorate degrees in political science at the University of Michigan.

2. *Muslim Pioneers in America*

One of the oldest Muslim communities in America is located in Willows, California, a few hundred miles north of San Francisco. Fazal Mohamed Khan, a leader in the Pakistan-American Association and several other Muslim groups, is an example of the success Pakistanis have found in this part of America.

Mr. Khan was born in the Punjab region in 1907 and came to America at the age of 16. He worked in the asparagus and rice fields of California. In 1929, with 2 partners, he began cultivation of 50 acres of rice. After restrictions against aliens' owning land were lifted in 1946, Mr. Khan's holdings rose to 2,500 acres. Today another 2,000 acres are leased by him for the production of rice. Fazal Mohamed Khan has become one of the most successful farmer-businessmen in the Sacramento Valley.

Sabu Dastagir was another Muslim who claimed Pakistan as his mother country, although he was born in South India. Sabu was born in 1924 in the Karapur jungle, 45 miles from Mysore. His father, who was an elephant trainer and hunting guide, died when Sabu was three. At the age of 12, Sabu was discovered by a director looking for an authentic cast for the movie *Elephant Boy.*

Sabu became famous for his part in this film. He played Abu in his second picture, *The Thief of Bagdad,* and then Mowgli in the movie version of Kipling's *Jungle Book.*

In 1944 Sabu received his American citizenship following enlistment in the Army Air Force. While in the service he flew 42 aerial missions as a B-24 gunner in the South Pacific and was awarded the Distinguished Flying Cross. He died in 1963 at only 39 years of age.

Sabu Dastagir appeared in *Elephant Boy* (1936) and many other adventure films.

Dr. Hafeez Malik, an authority on the Muslim world and Islamic studies, has enriched America's understanding of other cultures since he came here in 1953 to enter graduate school at Syracuse University. In Pakistan he had received a degree in journalism from the University of the Punjab and had been public relations officer for the city of Lahore.

From 1958 to 1961 Dr. Malik was White House correspondent for two Pakistani daily newspapers. He received his doctorate in political science from Syracuse in 1961. Since then he has been visiting professor in the Foreign Service Institute of the United States State Department. He is also a professor of political science at Villanova University in Pennsylvania. He speaks seven languages and has published four books and many papers in his field.

Dr. Farhataziz, a leading nuclear scientist from Pakistan, came to America in 1964. He was born in 1932 in Amritsar which is now in India. His childhood memories are those of a lower middle class family:

Dr. Hafeez Malik, professor of political science at Villanova University in Pennsylvania.

Dr. Farhataziz, a nuclear scientist, works at Notre Dame University's radiation laboratory.

The segregation of the white population (the British) as superior to the Indians, was difficult to accept. When I entered with my family into independent Pakistan it was a day of great human ecstasy . . . but the butchery of human beings on both sides was revolting. The clash between positives and negatives such as love and hatred often shaped my thinking. I grew up to accept and respect humanity as humanity—and not by its creed, nationality, clothing, colour, nor any other visual distinction.

Farhataziz graduated at the head of his class at Punjab University in 1953 and 1954. He received his doctorate in physical chemistry at Cambridge University in England in 1959. Under the sponsorship of the Pakistan Atomic Energy Commission he has worked as a radiation chemist in nuclear institutes in Iran, England, and Canada. Since 1964 Dr. Farhataziz has been doing research at the radiation laboratory of the University of Notre Dame in Indiana.

Anwar S. Dil, a student and teacher of linguistics and education at the University of Indiana.

Mr. and Mrs. Anwar S. Dil and their children are a student family who have done much to promote understanding and goodwill between Pakistan and America. Both Mr. and Mrs. Dil are, appropriately, students of language. They taught English and literature in Pakistan before coming to the United States in 1960 to study for masters degrees in applied linguistics at the University of Michigan. Now they are working for Ph.D.'s in linguistics and education at the University of Indiana. Mr. Dil organized the Pakistan Studies Group and the Pakistan Linguistic Research Group which has published eight books, attracting the attention of language scholars all over the world.

3. *Recent Residents*

American immigration quotas give preference to aliens with skills and professional backgrounds. Many Pakistanis who have become naturalized Americans are working in schools, colleges, and hospitals.

Immigrants Born in Pakistan
Admitted to the United States, 1948-1966

1948	2
1949	8
1950	10
1951	9
1952	4
1953	22
1954	85
1955	103
1956	118
1957	110
1958	152
1959	172
1960	154
1961	142
1962	169
1963	193
1964	155
1965	187
1966	1,781

Immigrants Born in India
Admitted to the United States, 1820-1966

1820-	1
1821-1830	8
1831-1840	39
1841-1850	36
1851-1860	43
1861-1870	69
1871-1880	163
1881-1890	269
1891-1900	68
1901-1910	4,713
1911-1920	2,082
1921-1930	1,886
1931-1940	496
1941-1950	1,761
1951-1960	1,973
1961	292
1962	390
1963	965
1964	488
1965	467
1966	7,560

Immigration from India and Pakistan increased tremendously in 1965-66 because of new, more lenient laws which select eligibles from Asia by skills, by relationship with persons already residing in America, and by filling unused quotas from other countries.

Aliens who reported under the alien address program from Pakistan numbered 653 in 1965. Most of these people live in New York or California, and a smaller community has settled in Detroit. Headquarters of the Pakistani League of America are located in New York.

The Pakistanis have built mosques, or Muslim places of worship, in New York, Detroit, San Francisco, Sacramento, and El Centro. The Sacramento Mosque has a membership of about 400. Women are allowed to enter and worship with the men, a practice unheard of in Pakistan. With the mosque as its center, Pakistanis form a very close community group. If possible they marry within their own group, or to an American who is of the Muslim faith or who will convert to the faith. When an older member of the group dies, his religious brothers provide financial assistance for burial rites, if necessary.

Fewer than 2,000 Pakistanis have come to America since 1947. Many have returned to Pakistan, for more than half of them were students. Since Pakistan is not quite 20 years old, all of her people in America are, in effect, pioneers.

The "Hindustan Club" at the University of California, Berkeley, in 1921. Note the great variety of facial types, from all over India. Few students came to America before Indian independence in 1947, but now they make up about one-third of the people coming from India.

PART VI

East Indian Immigration Since 1947

1. *The Students*

On August 15, 1947 India gained her independence from England. The world had entered an atomic, scientific age with which the newly independent country would have to keep pace. American schools offered technical knowledge and skills to India's youth.

Until this time only a few dozen students had come to American universities. By 1948, however, there were students from India in almost every state in America. Thousands of scholarships were offered by private and public foundations in both countries. Not all of the students were men. Women of India, now able to become doctors, teachers, and technicians, made the beauty of the sari evident on many campuses of the country.

49

Numerous young people were offered jobs on graduation and remained in the United States to marry and raise families. Others went back to India only to find that their newly-free homeland was not yet able to utilize their talents. So they returned to America and the advantages of a better income and higher standard of living. Over the years it has been found that more than half of India's students remain in or return to America.

Students make up about one-third of the people coming from India to America today. At the California Institute of Technology there are research fellows and professors in physics, chemical engineering, biology, materials science, geology, and electrical engineering. In the Boston area alone, there are 300 students from India doing graduate work at various universities. India's students have also been of valuable service to the Peace Corps. They have taught volunteers some of India's 16 languages.

Dr. Harbans L. Arora, a research biologist at Rockefeller Institute in New York.

Dr. Subrahmanyan Chandrasekhar, professor of astronomy and physics at the University of Chicago.

2. *Contributions in Science, Industry, and Medicine*

There are many scientists from India at work in America today on subjects and projects that are very important to our future. One of these men is Dr. Harbans L. Arora, a biologist born in Bharthanwala, a village now located in Pakistan. Dr. Arora has gained international attention as a research fellow at Rockefeller Institute with his experiments on the growth of optic nerve fibers and brain tissues of fishes. His work will tell us more about man's brain, his memory systems, and his behavior.

Another internationally recognized scientist from India is Dr. Subrahmanyan Chandrasekhar, associated with the Laboratory for Astrophysics and Space Research in Chicago. Dr. Chandrasekhar was educated in India and England and came to the United States in 1936. Since then he has served as editor of the *Astrophysics Journal* and has won numerous recognitions. His special field is the internal constitution of the stars and the dynamics and theory of stellar systems.

51

Dr. Har Gobind Khorana, professor and co-director of the Institute for Enzyme Research at the University of Wisconsin.

Dr. Har Gobind Khorana, born at Raipur in central India, came to the United States in 1958. He is one of the scientists who have solved the mysteries of the genetic code. As co-director of the Institute for Enzyme Research at the University of Wisconsin, his work teaches us more about cancer and infectious diseases and adds to our knowledge of the aging process.

Dr. C. Kumar N. Patel, who came to America from India less than 10 years ago, was the recent recipient of the Adolph Lomb Medal of the Optical Society of America. This medal is awarded to a person under 30 years of age who has made an outstanding contribution to the science of optics. Dr. Patel received the award for his pioneering research with lasers, devices which excite atoms so that they release stored energy as light. With these beams of stimulated light, man can bounce light off the surface of the moon or burn holes through sheets of steel.

Dr. Patel, the son of a civil engineer, was born in the state of Maharashtra, India in 1938. When he graduated from the College of Engineering at Poona University, lasers had not yet been discovered. Dr. Patel hopes that someday lasers may be used to cure cancer. He also sees a future for lasers in outerspace communication.

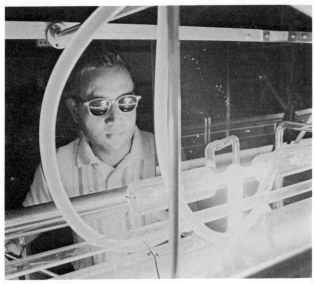

Dr. C. Kumar N. Patel does research in lasers at Bell Telephone Laboratories in New Jersey.

Dr. Narinder Singh Kapany, born in the Punjab in 1926, came to America in 1955. His training in physics and mathematics at Agra University led him to optics research in this country. The Watumull Foundation has recently awarded him honors for his invention of a laser instrument that performs an eye operation. Dr. Kapany has also invented a flexible bundle of photosensitive fibers with which a doctor can look inside the human body.

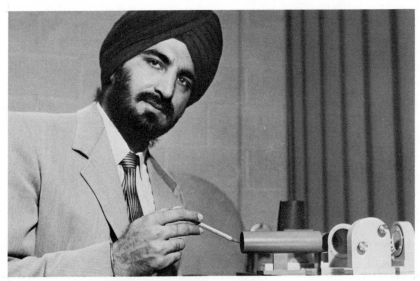

Dr. Narinder Singh Kapany, president and research director of an optics firm in California.

3. *Contributions in the Arts and Education*

The youngest conductor ever to lead a major symphony orchestra, Zubin Mehta, was born in Bombay to a prominent Parsee family. His father was an accomplished violinist, conductor, and founder of the Bombay Symphony Orchestra. Zubin grew up hearing the finest Western music.

In 1958 Zubin Mehta won an international contest for young conductors in Liverpool, England. Later he was guest conductor for the Vienna Philharmonic. After he came to the United States at the age of 24, he was appointed conductor of the Los Angeles Philharmonic Orchestra. One year later he became its music director. His romantic approach to conducting and his outstanding technical ability have been praised by critics and enjoyed by audiences in many nations.

Ravi Shankar, one of India's outstanding musicians, has popularized music of the *sitar*, a Hindu instrument resembling a guitar.

Zubin Mehta, music director of the Los Angeles Philharmonic Orchestra.

Ravi Shankar with his *sitar*.

He has influenced America jazz as well as popular music. Sitar accompaniment has been called "raga-rock." Mr. Shankar teaches sitar at the University of California's Los Angeles Department of Ethno-Musicology.

Ustad Ali Akbar Khan, India's preeminent master of the *sarod*, another stringed instrument, has made extensive tours of America. He now teaches the intricacies of this Eastern instrument at colleges throughout the United States.

Ustad Ali Akbar Khan plays the *sarod*.

An East Indian woman has a respected place in the field of American literature. Santha Rama Rau was born in South India, the daughter of an Indian diplomat. She has written seven books, a play, and numerous articles for magazines concerning her international background.

Ved Mehta, a staff member of the *New Yorker* magazine, was born in the Punjab region of India, the son of a distinguished doctor. At the age of three and a half he lost his eyesight after a long siege of illness. As he grew up, everyone but his father discouraged him from attempting to obtain an education beyond what is usually offered the blind.

Santha Rama Rau, (left) essayist and novelist. Her play, *A Passage to India,* from the novel by British writer E. M. Forster, was staged in London and New York in 1961-62. **Dr. Amiya Chakravarty** (right) teaches oriental religions and literature at Smith College.

Gopal Mitra, with an exhibit of his paintings at the Minneapolis Art Institute. Born in Patna, Bihar, Mr. Mitra came to America in 1958 to study art at the University of Minnesota, where he received a master's degree in Fine Arts and a doctorate in Art Education. An enthusiastic teacher, he attempts to unite the ideas and methods of India and America in his work.

At 15, after 30 rejections from schools in foreign countries, he was accepted by the Arkansas School for the Blind, in Little Rock, and later received a scholarship to Pomona College in Claremont, California. His autobiography, *Face to Face*, was published in 1957. He also studied at Balliol College, Oxford University, and wrote a series of articles for the *New Yorker* about modern British historians and philosophers which later appeared in book form, as have his stories about life in India.

Other Americans of East Indian descent have made important contributions in the field of education. One of them, Dr. Amiya Chakravarti, is a professor of oriental religions and literature at Smith College in Massachusetts. Dr. Chakravarti has been advisor to the Indian delegation of the General Assembly of the United Nations. He is the author of many books, one of which won the UNESCO prize in 1964.

Many American universities now have departments of Asian studies and are translating and publishing India's thousand year old classics of literature. Seven of the major universities in the United States sponsor the Rabindranath Tagore Memorial Lectureship (named after India's Nobel prize-winning poet) given annually on themes related to Indian civilization. The University of the Pacific in California will soon open a college of nonwestern studies with a branch in New Delhi.

4. *Contributions in Agriculture*

Today America's agricultural communities of East Indians have grown large and successful. There are over 50 families in Imperial Valley, California. Many of them are millionaires. Imperial Valley at times supplies 90 percent of the lettuce for the United States. In 1966 East Indian farmers produced 150 crates of cantaloupe an acre, compared to an average yield of 90 crates per acre. East Indians also raise cotton, sugar beets, alfalfa, barley, flax, tomatoes, and carrots.

The larger Sacramento Valley communities in California, which include hundreds of East Indian families, are no less successful. Using the latest in mechanized equipment, these hardworking farmers are at last dissociated from the famines of India — and are a major force in feeding America.

5. *Property and Business*

Since they were denied the right to own land until 1947, property ownership is a matter of pride to East Indians. In San Francisco East Indians own or lease more than 50 hotels, forming the second largest (next to the Sikh farmers) Indian community group in America. Most of the hotel owners are from Gujarat, a state on the west coast of India.

Although the farm and hotel communities are closely knit, it is interesting to note that the East Indians do not frown on marriage with Americans, nor have they formed closed communities. East Indians have been assimilated into their country and city surroundings. Their children are marrying Americans. Their enthusiasms have transferred from cricket to baseball.

East Indians are owners of machine shops, photo studios, restaurants, and many other successful businesses, including import-export firms and gift shops. America's appreciation of India's incense, brass, and silks has grown to include more sophisticated art objects now found in the most exclusive decorator showrooms. So many fragments of temple carvings, ancient wall hangings, and religious statuary have been brought from India that the government, fearful of losing its cultural heritage to collectors, has severely limited exports of these items.

Conclusion

Cumin, cloves, turmeric, fenugreek, coriander, cardamom — the spices that were so important in bringing about the discovery of America — are now abundant in most American grocery stores. East Indian and Pakistani foods have found a place in our daily lives. Lamb curry and tandouri chicken are on the menus of the finest restaurants. Mangoes are sold in American supermarkets, and yogurt has become a part of the American diet.

In recent years American designers and importers have discovered that the grace and comfort of Indian costume can be adapted to American dress. These Indian girls model the *sari* (left), and the *salwar chemise* (right) of North India

A version of the Pakistani dress for women, trousers and tunic, has been fashioned for sportswear. India's gilt and jeweled sandals and bracelets are also popular. The sari has been adapted to American evening dress.

Yoga has many enthusiasts in America. It is taught here as a form of exercise, while in India it is a form of spiritual discipline. The games of chess, parcheesi, and badminton originated in India during Muslim rule. Our word "punch" comes from the Indian word "panch" meaning "five." The area of the Punjab was thus named because of its five main rivers. To punch an object one needs five fingers gathered into a fist. To make a punch drink one needs five fingers to squeeze the orange.

But more important than food, fashion, or games are the people and ideas from India and Pakistan. They have added immeasurably to America's intellectual wealth. Gandhi's nonviolence may enable the American Negro to gain new status in education, voting, housing, and jobs. Centuries ago India gave the West the mathematical concept of zero. Now, India and Pakistan are giving America scientists who are improving and prolonging our lives, and extending our environment from earth to space.

. . . INDEX . . .

art *6, 7, 14, 57, 59*
Arora, Harbans L. *50*

Bagai, Kala Chandra *23*
British East India Company *16, 17*
British rule *9-11, 16-18, 29, 30, 35, 36, 41, 45, 49*

caste *10, 19-21, 30, 33*
Chakravarty, Amiya *56*
Chandrasekhar, Subrahmanyan *51*
Clive, Robert *16*
clothing *15, 22, 23, 27-29, 49, 59, 60*

Dastagir, Sabu *43*
Delhi *13, 17, 33*
Dil, Anwar S. *46*

Emerson, Ralph Waldo *8*
emigration, reasons for *18, 19, 28, 29, 33, 34, 36, 46, 49, 50*

Farhataziz *45*

Gandhi, Mohandas K. *9-12, 18, 34, 40, 60*
Gill, Sarwan Singh *15*

Hinduism *6, 8, 9, 11, 14, 15, 19-21, 23-27, 30, 41*
Hossain, Syud *34, 35*

immigration and naturalization laws, U. S. *22, 30-32, 35, 38, 39, 42, 46, 47, 58*
independence, movement for *9-11, 17, 18, 34, 35, 39, 41, 49*
Indian National Congress *17*

Jallianwala Bagh (Amritsar Massacre) *18, 29*
Jinnah, Mohammed Ali *41*

Kapany, Narinder Singh *53*
Kashmir *15, 41*

Khan, Fazal Mohamed *42*
Khan, Rais A. *42*
Khan, Ustad Ali Akbar *55*
Khorana, Har Gobind *52*
King, Martin Luther, Jr. *10*

Lal, Gobind Behari *33, 34*
Lincoln, Abraham *10, 12, 36*
Luce-Cellar Bill *31, 35, 37, 40*

Malik, Hafeez *44*
Mehta, Ved *56, 57*
Mehta, Zubin *54*
Mitra, Gopal *57*
Muslim League *41*
Muslims *13-15, 19, 22, 24, 34, 35, 41-48*

New Delhi *13, 58*
nonviolent resistance *9, 10, 11, 18*

occupations *21, 23, 28-30, 32, 34, 36, 38, 42-46, 50-60*

Pandit, Sakaram Ganesh *30-32*
partition *10, 13, 14, 28, 35, 39, 41, 45*
Patel, C. Kumar N. *52, 53*
Plassey, Battle of *16*

Rama Rau, Santha *56*
Ramakrishna *26*

Saund, Dalip Singh *35-37*
Sepoy Rebellion *17*
Shankar, Ravi *55*
Sikhs *15, 19, 23, 24, 28-30, 32, 58*

Thoreau, Henry David *9*

Vedanta *25-27*
Vivekananda, Swami *25-27*

Watumull Foundation *34, 39, 40, 53*
Watumull, Gobindram J. *37-40*
Whitman, Walt *8*

ACKNOWLEDGEMENTS

The illustrations are reproduced through the courtesy of: pp. 6, 14, The Denver Art Museum; p. 7, Museum of Fine Arts, Boston; p. 8, The Pennsylvania Academy of the Fine Arts; p. 9, Library of Congress; pp. 10, 11, 13, 16 (bottom), 17, 18, 20, 57, 60, Independent Picture Service; p. 12 (left), Post Office Department, Division of Philately; pp. 12 (right), 15, 46, 59, Leona B. Bagai; p. 16 (top), National Portrait Gallery, London; pp. 22, 23, 29, 31, 49, Films of India; pp. 25, 27, Vedanta Society of Southern California; p. 33, San Francisco Examiner; p. 36, E. P. Dutton & Co., Inc.; p. 39, First National Bank of Hawaii and Ansel Adams; p. 42, Clarion State College; p. 43, Universal Pictures; p. 44, Villanova University; p. 45, University of Notre Dame; p. 50, Rockefeller University; p. 51, University of Chicago; p. 52, University of Wisconsin; p. 53 (top), Bell Telephone Laboratories; p. 53 (bottom), Illinois Institute of Technology; p. 54, Los Angeles Philharmonic Orchestra; p. 55 (top), Jay K. Hoffman Presentations; p. 55 (bottom), American Society for Eastern Arts; p. 56 (left), Harper & Row, Publishers; p. 56 (right), Smith College.

ABOUT THE AUTHOR

Leona B. Bagai, author, editor, and critic, was born in Pennsylvania and spent her childhood in Cleveland, Ohio. A member of the *Los Angeles Times* Sunday Book Review staff for the past 10 years, she also reviews books on India for the *Chicago Tribune*, the *Pasadena Independent-Star News* and the University of Oklahoma's literary quarterly, *Books Abroad*. For two years she was editor of the *India-America Society Bulletin*. With her husband, who was born in Peshawar (now a part of Pakistan), she wrote the English scenario, subtitles, and song lyrics for an East Indian motion picture, *Two Eyes, Twelve Hands*, and produced a record album entitled *The Great Music of India*. The Bagais and their four children live in Los Angeles.

Mrs. Bagai's mother-in-law, a Sikh, was one of the seven pioneer East Indian women to come to America before World War I. Her father-in-law, a Hindu, attained American citizenship early in the century and was an ardent worker for India's freedom.

The IN AMERICA *Series*

The CZECHS *and* SLOVAKS *in America*
The EAST INDIANS *and* PAKISTANIS *in Americ*
The ENGLISH *in America*
The FRENCH *in America*
The GERMANS *in America*
The IRISH *in America*
The ITALIANS *in America*
The JAPANESE *in America*
The NEGRO *in America*
The NORWEGIANS *in America*
The SCOTS *and* SCOTCH-IRISH *in America*
The SWEDES *in America*
The FREEDOM OF THE PRESS *in America*
The FREEDOM OF SPEECH *in America*

We specialize in publishing quality books for
young people. For a complete list please write:

LERNER PUBLICATIONS COMPANY
241 First Avenue North, Minneapolis, Minnesota 55401